DIPS

DIPS

More than 65 delicious recipes for snacking, sharing and more

RYLAND PETERS & SMALL

Designer Paul Stradling
Editor Abi Waters
Head of Production Patricia Harrington
Indexer Vanessa Bird

Published in 2026 by
Ryland Peters & Small
20–21 Jockey's Fields
London WC1R 4BW

www.rylandpeters.com
email: euregulations@rylandpeters.com

10 9 8 7 6 5 4 3 2 1

ISBN: 978-1-78879-777-1

Printed in China.

A CIP record for this book is available from the British Library.
US Library of Congress Cataloging-in-Publication data has been applied for.

The authorised representative in the EEA is Authorised Rep Compliance Ltd., Ground Floor, 71 Lower Baggot Street, Dublin, D02 P593, Ireland.
www.arccompliance.com

NOTES

• Both British (Metric) and American (Imperial ounces plus US cups) are included in these recipes for your convenience; however, it is important to work with one set of measurements only and not alternate between the two within a recipe.

• All spoon measurements are level unless otherwise specified.

• All eggs are medium (UK) or large (US), unless specified as large, in which case US extra-large should be used. Uncooked or partially cooked eggs should not be served to the very old, frail, young children, pregnant women or those with compromised immune systems.

• Ovens should be preheated to the specified temperatures. We recommend using an oven thermometer. If using a fan-assisted oven, adjust temperatures according to the manufacturer's instructions.

• When a recipe calls for the grated zest of citrus fruit, buy unwaxed fruit and wash well before using. If you can only find treated fruit, scrub well in warm soapy water before using.

FSC www.fsc.org
MIX
Paper | Supporting responsible forestry
FSC® C008047

CONTENTS

INTRODUCTION

Dips are the quiet heroes of the table. They have an amazing ability to bring people together, turn simple ingredients into something very special and make every snack feel like a celebration.

Inside these pages you'll find dips for every mood, moment and craving. We begin with Return of the Dip, a tribute to the classics that have earned their place at the table time and time again. These are the familiar favourites – comforting, reliable and always crowd-pleasing. The dips you'll reach for again and again as a fail-safe option.

Next comes Clean Dippin', where bright flavours and fresh ingredients take the spotlight. These lighter dips are vibrant and refreshing and perfect when you want something satisfying without feeling too overly indulgent. They are the everyday dips that will suit all occasions.

For those moments when only pure indulgence will do, Dip Decadence dives into rich, luxurious creations. Creamy, bold and unapologetically satisfying, these dips are made to impress and delight. Strong flavours, luxury ingredients and ultimate satisfaction are the name of the game here.

Sometimes, though, the best dips are the ones that arrive warm and bubbling straight from the oven. Dip It Like It's Hot is dedicated to those gooey, melty dishes that fill the room with irresistible aromas and enticing flavours and disappear almost as quickly as they're served.

When it's time to entertain, Dip, Dip, Hooray brings together a collection of crowd-friendly dips designed for sharing, celebrating and keeping guests coming back for 'just one more scoop'.

Of course, every great dip deserves the perfect partner. In Chip, Dip, Repeat, you'll find a selection of crackers, chips, breads and other dunkers designed to complement every bowl.

So whether it's a bowl placed at the centre of a party or a quick spread prepared for a quiet night in watching TV, a good dip has a way of bringing everyone together to scoop, savour and enjoy. This cookbook celebrates that irresistible magic – one scoop at a time.

Grab a chip, tear some bread or slice some veggies, because the best way to enjoy this book is to dive right in.

RETURN OF THE DIP

Classic dips for every occasion

CLASSIC HUMMUS

This hugely popular tasty, nutty-flavoured Middle Eastern dip is so easy to make at home. Serve it with pitta bread, falafel or vegetable crudités as a snack or alongside other mezze dishes for a light meal.

125 g/¾ cup dried chickpeas/ garbanzo beans

1 tsp bicarbonate of soda/ baking soda

2 garlic cloves, peeled and crushed to a paste in a mortar with a pestle

4 tbsp tahini

juice of 1 lemon

salt

toasted or griddled pitta bread, to serve

TO GARNISH

extra virgin olive oil

paprika or sumac

finely chopped fresh flat-leaf parsley

SERVES 4–6

Soak the chickpeas overnight in plenty of cold water with the bicarbonate of soda.

Next day, drain and rinse. Put in a large pan, add enough fresh cold water to cover well and bring to the boil. Reduce the heat and simmer for 50–60 minutes until tender, skimming off any scum. Season the chickpeas with salt, then drain, reserving the cooking water and setting aside 1 tablespoon of the cooked chickpeas for the garnish.

In a food processor, blend together the cooked chickpeas, garlic, tahini and lemon juice. Gradually add the cooking liquid until the mixture becomes a smooth paste. Season with salt. Transfer the hummus to a serving bowl.

To serve, make a shallow hollow in the centre of the hummus using the back of a spoon. Pour in a little olive oil, top with the reserved whole chickpeas, a sprinkle of paprika or sumac and the chopped parsley. Serve with toasted or griddled pitta bread.

BEETROOT HUMMUS

This is the dip for you if you want to take the classic hummus one step further. Serve with squid ink crackers – the rich red of the hummus works beautifully with the dramatic black of the crackers, and the slightly sweet and salty flavour combination is absolutely stunning.

140 g/1 cup canned chickpeas/garbanzo beans, drained and rinsed

250 g/2 scant cups beetroot/beets, cooked and cubed

1 large garlic clove, peeled

2 tbsp olive oil

1 tbsp lemon juice

2 tbsp tahini

2–3 pinches of sea salt flakes

pea shoots (or other micro herbs), to garnish

Squid Ink Crackers (see page 125), to serve

SERVES 4–6

To make the hummus, put all of the ingredients in a food processor or blender and blitz until smooth. Taste and adjust the seasoning, if necessary.

Spoon the hummus into a bowl, garnish with a few pea shoots and serve with the squid ink crackers for dipping.

Tip: If you want to use dried chickpeas and soak and cook them yourself before making the hummus, follow the instructions on page 11.

TOMATO SALSA

opposite, bottom

When these fresh, simple ingredients are combined together, they produce a wonderful salsa bursting with flavour. Like other Mexican salsas, there are many variations, such as adding lime juice and fresh chillies. Because it's not spicy, it can be enjoyed by kids as well.

4 tomatoes

¼ onion

bunch of fresh coriander/cilantro

¼ tsp sea salt

MAKES A BOWLFUL

Finely chop the tomatoes, onion and coriander and place in a bowl. Add the salt and mix well.

Tip: Next time you make this mild salsa, feel free to adjust the proportions according to your taste.

GUACAMOLE

opposite, top

One of the most widely known side dishes in Mexican cooking outside of Mexico, guacamole was made as early as the 16th century by the Aztec people. There are numerous variations, but the recipe below allows the flavour and texture of the avocado to shine through.

2–3 avocados

bunch of fresh coriander/cilantro

1 tomato

pinch of sea salt

pinch of ground white pepper

MAKES A BOWLFUL

Pit and peel the avocados. Scoop the flesh out into a bowl. Finely chop the coriander and add to the bowl with the salt and pepper. Roughly mash with a fork.

Finely chop the tomato and stir into the guacamole.

TARAMASALATA

This delicious Greek dip is easier to make from scratch than you might think. Using a decent blender is key, as the texture should be smooth and light. Serve with olives and plenty of toasted pitta bread for a snack, or as part of a mezze feast with other dips and small plates.

200 g/7 oz. can cod roe, drained

1 small red onion, grated

½ tsp cayenne pepper, plus extra, to taste

2 tbsp lemon juice, plus extra, to taste

1 chunky slice of toasted bread

50 ml/3½ tbsp milk

100 ml/7 tbsp extra virgin olive oil, plus extra to serve

salt and black pepper

TO SERVE

olives

toasted pitta bread

MAKES ABOUT 500 G/2 CUPS

Add the drained cod roe to a food processor, breaking it up with the back of a fork, then add the grated onion, cayenne pepper and lemon juice and season generously with salt and black pepper.

Soak the toasted bread in the milk for a minute, then squeeze out the excess liquid and tear the toast into the food processor (discard the leftover milk). Pulse everything in the food processor to begin with, then increase the speed and start drizzling in the olive oil until it has all been added.

Add a couple of tablespoons of water at the end to smooth the taramasalata if needed. Taste, adding more salt, lemon juice or cayenne as preferred.

Serve in a bowl with a little extra drizzle of olive oil, a few olives alongside and some toasted pitta bread for dipping.

BABA GHANOUSH

Serve this traditional Middle Eastern-style dip with smoked paprika-dusted pitta chips as a vegetarian appetizer, or with other dishes, such as Classic Hummus (see page 11) or Tzatziki (see page 23), as part of a bountiful mezze spread.

2 aubergines/eggplants

2 garlic cloves, peeled

juice of ½ lemon

3 tbsp extra virgin olive oil, plus extra to serve

sea salt

pomegranate seeds, to garnish (optional)

Paprika Pitta Chips (see page 118), to serve

SERVES 4–6

Preheat the oven to 200°C (400°F) Gas 6.

Put the aubergines on a foil-lined baking sheet and roast in the preheated oven for 1 hour, turning over halfway through, until charred on all sides.

Put the hot aubergines in a plastic bag (so that the resulting steam will make the skin easier to peel off) and set aside to cool.

Once cool, peel the roasted aubergines and chop the flesh into chunks. Pound the garlic in a mortar with a pestle (with a pinch of salt) until it is a paste.

In a food processor, blend the roast aubergines, garlic paste, lemon juice and olive oil to a smooth purée. Season with salt and cover until ready to serve.

Put the dip in a serving bowl and sprinkle with pomegranate seeds, if using. Drizzle with extra virgin olive oil and serve with the paprika pitta chips on the side for dipping.

MUHAMMARA

3 large red (bell) peppers

1 slice of day-old sourdough bread, cut into small pieces

100 g/3½ oz. walnut halves, coarsely chopped

½ tsp dried red chilli/hot pepper flakes

1 tbsp sun-dried tomato paste

2 garlic cloves, peeled and chopped

2 tsp lemon juice

1 tbsp balsamic vinegar

2 tsp caster/granulated sugar

1 tsp ground cumin

2 tbsp olive oil, plus extra to drizzle

sea salt and black pepper

TO SERVE

chopped pistachios

toasted pitta or other flatbread

SERVES 6–8

This dip is made from roasted red (bell) peppers and earthy walnuts, with a little kick of spice. Its vibrant colour and tangy flavour provide a wonderful contrast to creamier dips when served together.

Cook the peppers one at a time by skewering each one on a fork and holding it directly over a gas flame for 10–15 minutes, until the skin is blackened all over. Alternatively, put them on a baking sheet in an oven preheated to 220°C (425°F) Gas 7. Cook them for about 10–15 minutes, until the skin has puffed up and blackened all over. Transfer to a bowl, cover with cling film/plastic wrap and leave until cool enough to handle.

Using your hands, remove the skin and seeds from the peppers and tear the flesh into pieces. Put the flesh in a food processor and add the remaining ingredients. Process to a coarse paste. Season to taste and transfer to a bowl. Cover with cling film and refrigerate for 8 hours or ideally overnight before serving.

To serve, bring the dip to room temperature and transfer it to a shallow bowl. Drizzle with olive oil and sprinkle with chopped pistachios. Serve with toasted pitta or flatbread.

TZATZIKI *opposite, bottom*

A Greek classic, this creamy combination of yogurt, cucumber and fresh dill is so simple to make but uniquely refreshing.

1 large, firm cucumber

½ tsp salt, plus 2 pinches

400 g/2 scant cups Greek/ US strained plain yogurt

2 tbsp chopped fresh dill, plus extra to garnish (optional)

2 garlic cloves, peeled and crushed

1 tbsp olive oil

SERVES 4–6

Peel, deseed and dice the cucumber. Reserve a little to garnish. Sprinkle the rest with ½ teaspoon salt, mix well and set aside for 5 minutes.

Wrap the cucumber in a spotlessly clean kitchen towel and squeeze to remove the liquid. Put the cucumber in a bowl, then add the remaining ingredients. Mix together well and serve, garnished with the reserved cucumber and dill, if you like.

Variations

Beetroot/Beet Tzatziki Add 1 medium raw grated beetroot/beet and 2 tablespoons chopped chives to the mixture.

Olive Tzatziki Stir 100 g/¾–1 cup finely chopped pitted black or green olives into the mixture.

Also pictured: Roast Carrot, Ginger & Miso Dip; see page 42 for recipe.

RED PEPPER & FETA DIP

This is a traditional Greek dip of roasted (bell) peppers with tangy feta. Fresh tomato is added here to bring a sweet sharpness, but if you want something a little more sultry, you can use sun-dried tomatoes instead.

2 red (bell) peppers, halved, pith and seeds removed

4 garlic cloves, unpeeled

4 sprigs of fresh thyme

4 tbsp olive oil, plus extra for drizzling

few drops of lemon juice

small pinch of cayenne pepper

1 ripe vine tomato (or 2 baby plum tomatoes)

100 g/3½ oz. feta cheese, crumbled

1 tbsp finely chopped fresh flat-leaf parsley

salt and black pepper

SERVES 6

Preheat the oven to 200°C (400°F) Gas 6.

Place the pepper halves onto a baking sheet with a garlic clove and sprig of thyme under each one. Drizzle with olive oil, season with a little salt and pepper and roast in the oven for 20–25 minutes, until they start to char.

Squeeze the roasted garlic cloves out of their skins and drop them into the cup of a blender, followed by the roasted peppers (discarding the thyme), 2 tablespoons of olive oil, the lemon juice, cayenne pepper and tomato. Blend to a pulp.

Pour out the mixture, add the crumbled feta, the remaining 2 tablespoons of olive oil and the chopped parsley, and fold through. Serve.

Tip: Like many dips, this one also works really well as a marinade on meat, fish or veggies.

BROAD BEAN & CHICORY DIP

This soft, creamy mixture of puréed dried broad/fava beans is found in Puglia, southern Italy, where it is called *'ncapriata* or *fave e cicoria*. A similar dish called *macco* is served in Sicily, where it is often mixed with wild fennel. Make sure you use split beans that are already shelled, so you can skip that laborious task.

250 g/1⅓ cups split dried broad/fava beans

1 potato, peeled and diced

100 ml/½ cup olive oil, plus extra for frying

500 g/1 lb. chicory/endive

2 garlic cloves, crushed

salt

extra virgin olive oil, to drizzle

toasted sourdough bread, to serve

SERVES 4–6

In a large saucepan, boil the beans and potato in enough water to cover them by 4 cm/2 inches for about 1 hour. Add more boiling water during cooking if the mixture gets too dry. By the time the beans are cooked, most of the water should have been absorbed. Beat in the olive oil until you have a thick, smooth purée, then season well with salt.

Meanwhile, boil or steam the chicory. While cooking, heat a tablespoon of olive oil in a frying pan/skillet, and gently sauté the garlic, then toss the drained chicory in the garlicky oil.

To serve, spoon the dip into a bowl and top with the garlicky chicory. Drizzle with some good olive oil and serve with slices of toasted sourdough bread.

SMOKED SALMON, HORSERADISH & DILL DIP

Salmon and horseradish are a match made in heaven, and they pair perfectly in this creamy dip. You can adjust the lemon juice to your taste, adding a little more for a really zingy dip.

200 g/7 oz. smoked salmon slices

juice of 1 lemon

250 ml/1 cup crème fraîche or sour cream

1 tbsp chopped fresh dill, plus extra to serve

125 g/4½ oz. cream cheese

1 tbsp creamed horseradish

black pepper

Bagel Toasts (see page 119), warmed, to serve

SERVES 4

Reserve a piece of smoked salmon for garnish, then blitz the rest into small pieces in a food processor or blender with the lemon juice. Add the crème fraîche, dill, cream cheese and creamed horseradish and season with freshly ground black pepper. Smoked salmon is quite salty so you shouldn't need to add salt. Blitz for a few seconds until everything is combined.

Spoon into a bowl and garnish with the reserved salmon and some more dill sprigs.

Serve the dip with warm bagel toasts on the side.

Variation

Smoked Salmon, Caper & Red Onion Dip

Try replacing the dill and horseradish with a few spoonfuls of drained and chopped capers and some very finely chopped red onion.

QUICK CHILLI LIME MAYO

opposite, top

This is a hot and fruity mayonnaise that literally takes seconds to make. It's great with any seafood and does wonders for a posh tuna sandwich!

4 tbsp mayonnaise

grated zest and juice of 1 small lime

1 Scotch Bonnet chilli/chile, very finely chopped

MAKES 4 TBSP

Mix the mayonnaise and lime juice in a small bowl. Add the Scotch Bonnet, little by little, until the desired hotness is achieved. Garnish with lime zest.

FRESH AÏOLI

opposite, bottom left

This popular dip is lovely with potatoes or anything barbecued/grilled, especially prawns/shrimp or chicken. This recipe has a wonderful, robust garlicky flavour, not for the faint-hearted.

2 large egg yolks

4 very fresh garlic cloves, crushed

1 tsp Dijon mustard

150 ml/⅔ cup good-quality light olive oil

juice of ½ lemon

sea salt and black pepper

MAKES ABOUT 200 ML/¾ CUP

Beat the egg yolks in a large bowl with a balloon whisk. Add the garlic and mustard and beat through. While beating the mixture, slowly add the olive oil in a thin, steady stream. When all the oil has been added, the aïoli should have a smooth, velvety appearance.

Add the lemon juice, season with salt and pepper and gently stir through. Refrigerate until ready to serve.

ROAST GARLIC & CHIPOTLE MAYO *bottom right*

This tasty mayonnaise is really big on flavour. It's just right for alternative egg mayonnaise sandwiches or an amazing potato salad.

2 large garlic cloves, skin on
4 tbsp mayonnaise
½ tsp crushed chipotle chilli

MAKES 4 TBSP

Preheat the oven to 180°C (350°F) Gas 4.

Roast the garlic on a baking sheet in the preheated oven for 20 minutes until soft but not burnt. Remove from the oven and let cool for 10 minutes.

Squeeze the garlic from its skin into a small bowl. Gently mash with a fork. Add the mayonnaise and chipotle and stir until evenly mixed. Cover and refrigerate for 2–3 hours to let the chipotle rehydrate a little in the mayonnaise. Stir occasionally while it's chilling.

BLACK OLIVE TAPENADE

Classic Mediterranean ingredients are combined here to make a simple yet flavoursome dip. Serve with crusty bread and crudités.

1 garlic clove, crushed

juice of 1 lemon

3 tbsp capers, chopped

6 anchovy fillets, chopped

250 g/9 oz. black olives, pitted

leaves from a small bunch of fresh flat-leaf parsley, chopped

2–4 tbsp extra virgin olive oil

salt and black pepper

crusty bread and crudités, to serve

SERVES 4

Tip the garlic, lemon juice, capers and anchovies into a food processor and process for about 10 seconds.

Add the olives and parsley with just enough olive oil to make a paste and blitz again. Season to taste if needed.

Scrape out into a small bowl and serve with crusty bread and crudités. The dip has a very strong flavour so a little goes a long way!

DUKKAH

An Egyptian nut, seed and spice dip, dukkah is eaten with bread dunked in olive oil so that the delicious mix clings to it.

20 g/1½ tbsp blanched hazelnuts

20 g/1½ tbsp blanched almonds

1 tbsp cumin seeds

1 tbsp coriander seeds

2 tbsp sesame seeds

1 tbsp dried mint

¼ tsp salt

TO SERVE

extra virgin olive oil

chunks of crusty white bread

SERVES 4

Preheat the oven to 180°C (350°F) Gas 4.

Roast the nuts on separate baking sheets; the hazelnuts for about 5 minutes and the almonds for about 8 minutes. Leave to cool.

Meanwhile, in a dry frying pan/skillet set over a medium heat, fry the cumin seeds and coriander seeds for 1–2 minutes, until fragrant.

In a food processor, blitz the spices, roasted nuts, seeds, dried mint and salt until finely ground. Be careful not to blend for too long as the nuts will begin to release their oils and it will turn into a paste.

Carefully spoon the mixture into a bowl. Serve with a dish of olive oil and chunks of bread for dipping.

CLEAN DIPPIN'

Light & fresh dips for every day

PEA, FETA & MINT DIP

This dip is ideal for serving at an al fresco summer lunch. It is light and creamy with a perfect saltiness from the feta, and hints of lemon and mint make it really refreshing.

250g/9 oz. frozen peas

3 sprigs of fresh mint

grated zest and juice of 1 lemon

200g/7 oz. feta cheese

150g/5½ oz. cream cheese

salt and black pepper

TO SERVE

peashoots, to garnish (optional)

olive oil

Paprika Pitta Chips (see page 118) or Bagel Toasts (see page 119)

SERVES 4

Bring a saucepan of water to the boil and simmer the peas with the mint and a pinch of salt for about 5 minutes until cooked. Drain and blanch in cold water until the peas are cold.

Drain the peas and add to a blender with the mint and the lemon juice. Blitz to a purée but keep some texture to it. If you prefer a very smooth dip you can pass the pea mixture through a fine mesh sieve/strainer using a rubber spatula or spoon.

Crumble the feta into a mixing bowl, then whisk together with the cream cheese until smooth. Add the lemon zest, pea purée and a good grinding of black pepper and whisk again.

Spoon into a bowl and garnish with peashoots, if using, and a drizzle of olive oil. Serve with paprika pitta chips or bagel toasts for dipping.

FLAX-SPECKLED HUMMUS
WITH KALE CRISPS/CHIPS

400 g/3 cups cooked chickpeas/ garbanzo beans

2 tbsp tahini

juice of 2 large lemons

2 garlic cloves, crushed

1 tsp ground cumin

1 tbsp flaxseed oil

1 tbsp milled flaxseeds

salt and black pepper

KALE CRISPS/CHIPS

1 head of curly kale

2 tbsp olive oil

1 tbsp Parmesan cheese or nutritional yeast flakes if you are dairy-free

1 tsp onion powder or 2 small chopped onions

½ tsp Himalayan salt

SERVES 4

This nutrient-boosted hummus has a double dose of flax using both flaxseeds and flaxseed oil, so it's a great source of omega-3s. Kale, one of the best green superfoods, is delicious as a crisp/chip for dipping.

Place all of the ingredients for the hummus in a food processor with 2 tablespoons water and blend until a smooth consistency.

For the kale crisps, preheat the oven to 95°C (200°F) Gas ¼.

Wash and dry the kale. Mix the oil, Parmesan or nutritional yeast flakes, onion powder or chopped onion and salt in a bowl. Add the kale leaves to the bowl and coat with the oil mixture. Put the kale leaves on a baking sheet and cook in the preheated oven for 45 minutes. Keep an eye on them so as not to burn the edges.

Cool and serve with the hummus or store in an airtight container for up to 3 days.

WHITE BEAN & SPINACH DIP

This is a beautifully light and nutritious green dip that looks great garnished with fresh herbs and served with crunchy crostini.

410 g/2½ cups cooked white beans, drained

juice of 1 lemon

juice of 1 small orange

1 garlic clove, peeled

3 tbsp flaxseed oil

50 g/2 oz. spinach leaves

salt and black pepper

Crostini (see page 119), to serve

SERVES 4–6

Blend the beans, juices, garlic and oil in a food processor until blended but still chunky in texture.

Coarsely chop the spinach and stir into the dip mixture. Season to taste with salt and freshly ground black pepper.

Spoon the dip into a bowl and serve with the crostini on the side.

SPICED BEETROOT DIP

Beetroot/beet is as nutritious as it is colourful and makes a wonderfully flavourful dip. Sumac is a versatile North African and Middle Eastern spice, also used in the spice blend za'atar, which works beautifully with the earthiness of beetroot.

2 garlic bulbs, unpeeled

4 beetroot/beets, tops and bottoms trimmed

3 tbsp flaxseed oil

1½ tsp ground sumac

1 tsp cumin seeds

juice of 1 lemon

1 tsp sea salt

black pepper, to taste

handful of fresh coriander/cilantro, to garnish

Seeded Amaranth Crackers (see page 125), to serve

SERVES 4

Preheat the oven to 180°C (350°F) Gas 4. Line a baking sheet with parchment paper.

Wrap the garlic in foil and put on the prepared baking sheet. Wrap the beetroot in a separate sheet of foil and put on the same baking sheet. Roast the beetroot and garlic for about 30 minutes in the preheated oven, then remove the garlic and set aside. Roast the beetroot for a further 30 minutes or until tender, then allow to cool.

Peel the garlic and the beetroot (this is the messy part so feel free to wear gloves!) and blend them in a food processor with the flaxseed oil, sumac, cumin seeds, lemon juice, salt and pepper. Add more flaxseed oil as needed to reach the desired consistency.

Transfer the dip to a serving bowl, garnish with fresh coriander and serve with the crackers.

ROAST CARROT, GINGER & MISO DIP

pictured on page 22, top

Roasted carrots make a deliciously creamy and sweet dip. The ginger adds a welcome spicy heat and kick and the miso (fermented soya bean paste) adds a moreish savoury note.

300 g/10½ oz. sweet carrots, peeled and thinly sliced

25 g/1 oz. grated fresh ginger

3 tbsp white miso paste

2 tbsp tahini

black and white sesame seeds, to garnish (optional)

Homemade Tortilla Chips (see page 118) or plain crackers, to serve

SERVES 4

Preheat the oven to 180°C (350°F) Gas 4.

Put the carrots in a roasting pan and roast in the preheated oven for 20–25 minutes until softened but not browned. Set aside until cool.

Blitz the cooled carrots in a food processor or blender together with the ginger, miso and tahini. Spoon into a bowl, garnish with a sprinkling of sesame seeds, if using, and serve with tortilla chips or plain crackers.

EDAMAME & WASABI DIP

Edamame (soy) beans are a rare plant source of omega-3 fatty acids, so this delicious green dip packs a nutritional punch as well as making a lighter alternative to hummus.

200 g/1½ cups shelled edamame beans (fresh, or frozen and thawed)

3 tbsp sweet white miso paste

1 tbsp extra virgin olive oil

1 tbsp tamari soy sauce

1 tsp wasabi paste

vegetable crudités or breadsticks, to serve

SERVES 2–3

Put most of the edamame beans (reserving some to garnish) and 1 tablespoon water in a food processor and blitz until smooth. Add the remaining ingredients and mix well so that everything is well incorporated.

Spoon into a bowl, top with the reserved edamame beans and serve with crudités or breadsticks.

SPINACH HUMMUS

This vibrant dip is a great way to get more greens into your diet. Green leafy vegetables can lose nutrients if they are over-cooked. To avoid this, they can be used raw, like in this recipe. All the nutrients remain and the hummus becomes a beautiful green.

320 g/2 cups cooked chickpeas/ garbanzo beans, plus 60 ml/ ¼ cup of the cooking liquid, or more if needed

3 tbsp extra virgin olive oil

1 tbsp cashew butter

3 garlic cloves

1 tbsp umeboshi vinegar (optional)

70 g/1 handful raw spinach leaves

juice of ½ lemon, or to taste

½ tsp salt, or to taste

chopped fresh flat-leaf parsley, to garnish (optional)

Vegetable Crisps/Chips (see page 123), to serve

SERVES 2–3

Blend all the ingredients in a blender or food processor, slowly adding the cooking liquid until you reach a thick and creamy consistency; this will take about 1 minute.

Adjust the lemon juice and salt to taste. Garnish with chopped flat-leaf parsley, if you like, and serve with vegetable crisps/chips for dipping.

Tip: High-speed blenders will make the creamiest texture for this dip and need less liquid and time, but both food processors and stick blenders can be used as well.

BROAD BEAN & RICOTTA DIP

This dip has a fresh, pleasant nutty taste. Serve with strips of warm toasted pitta bread or vegetable crudités.

250 g/9 oz. fresh or frozen broad/fava beans

2 garlic cloves, crushed

1 tbsp olive oil

100 g/½ cup ricotta cheese

2 tbsp chopped fresh dill, plus extra to garnish

salt and black pepper

toasted pitta bread or crudités, to serve

SERVES 4

Preheat the oven to 180°C (350°F) Gas 4.

Cook the beans in a saucepan of boiling water until just tender. Drain, cool and pop the beans out of their skins.

Put the skinned beans, garlic and olive oil in a food processor and blend together; alternatively mash together in a bowl using a fork. Add the ricotta, chopped dill, salt and pepper and mix briefly.

Spoon the dip into a bowl, garnish with dill fronds and serve with warm toasted pitta bread or crudités.

ZESTY ALMOND & HERB PESTO

opposite, top

Traditionally, pesto is made with basil, pine nuts and Parmesan, but this cheese-free version is made with a mixture of fresh green herbs and almonds.

- 20 g/¾ oz. fresh baby spinach leaves
- leaves from 1 small bunch each fresh mint, flat-leaf parsley and coriander/cilantro
- 30 g/¼ cup blanched almonds
- 6 tbsp extra virgin olive oil
- 1 kaffir lime leaf
- juice of 1 lime
- grated zest of 1 lemon
- 1 garlic clove, peeled
- pinch of sea salt
- vegetable crudités or breadsticks, to serve

SERVES 2

Put all the ingredients in a food processor and blitz until they form a paste.

Spoon into a dish and serve immediately with crudités, such as carrot and cucumber batons, or breadsticks, for dipping. (Be aware that the herbs will oxidize and the dip will lose its vibrant green colour fairly quickly after making so it's important to serve it very fresh.)

LIGHTER GUACAMOLE

opposite, bottom

Although traditional guacamole is made with fresh healthy ingredients, it does have a high calorie content. This version has been lightened with the inclusion of fresh peas and (bell) peppers. It keeps its creamy texture and body, but makes it a lighter option.

- 1 large avocado, peeled and pitted
- 90 g/3 oz. peas (ideally fresh, but frozen and thawed is fine too)
- ½ red (bell) pepper, deseeded
- 2 tomatoes
- ¼ small onion
- 1 garlic clove, peeled
- large handful of fresh coriander/cilantro
- juice of ½ lime
- 1 tbsp lemon juice
- vegetable crudités or breadsticks, to serve

SERVES 2

Put all the ingredients in a food processor and blitz until smooth.

Spoon into a dish and serve immediately with crudités, such as carrot and cucumber batons, or breadsticks, for dipping. (Be aware that the avocado will quickly brown and the dip will lose its vibrant green colour fairly quickly after making so it's important to serve it very fresh.)

LIGHT AUBERGINE DIP
WITH ALMOND CHIA CRACKERS

800 g/2 large aubergines/ eggplants

2 tbsp grapeseed oil

½ tsp Himalayan salt

2 garlic cloves

2 tbsp lemon juice

3 tbsp flaxseed oil

salt and black pepper

ALMOND CHIA CRACKERS

60 g/½ cup almond flour

30 g/¼ cup coconut flour

30 g/¼ cup ground chia seeds

¾ tsp salt

½ tsp onion powder or 1 chopped small onion

60 ml/¼ cup olive oil

SERVES 2 (MAKES 12 CRACKERS)

This recipe is similar to the well-known Levantine dip, baba ghanoush, which traditionally contains tahini. Here, the tahini has been left out to let the pure flavour of the roasted aubergine/eggplant take centre stage. It goes beautifully well with the nutty almond chia crackers.

For the dip, preheat the oven to 200°C (400°F) Gas 6.

Cut the aubergines in half and pierce the skin and flesh several times. Put on a baking sheet, drizzle with grapeseed oil, sprinkle with salt and bake skin side up in the oven for 35–40 minutes, or until the flesh is tender. Remove from the oven and cool in a bowl of iced water. This will make it easier to peel away the skins.

Peel and discard the skins and add the flesh to the garlic, lemon juice and flaxseed oil in a food processor. Blend, season with salt and pepper and refrigerate until you are ready to serve.

For the crackers, preheat the oven to 180°C (350°F) Gas 4.

Add all of the dry ingredients to a mixing bowl. Add the oil and 60 ml/¼ cup water and mix to form a ball

with your hands. Chill in the refrigerator in cling film/plastic wrap for 20 minutes.

Roll out the dough thinly on a non-stick baking sheet. Bake in the preheated oven for 15 minutes, then remove from the oven, leave to cool and cut into 12 pieces.

Transfer the dip to a serving bowl and serve with the crackers.

AVOCADO MISO DIP WITH DUKKAH

This guacamole with a Japanese twist is so quick and easy to make and the dukkah, an Egyptian nut, seed and spice mix, adds a delicious texture to this snack attack.

120 g/4 oz. avocado, peeled and pitted

1 tbsp brown rice miso paste

1 tbsp lemon juice

2 tsp tahini

2 tsp extra virgin olive oil

1 small garlic clove, crushed

Dukkah (see page 31), for sprinkling

Vegetable Crisps/Chips (see page 123), to serve

SERVES 2

Preheat the oven to 180°C (350°F) Gas 4.

Blitz the avocado in the food processor with the miso paste, lemon juice, tahini, olive oil and garlic until smooth. Taste and adjust the seasoning if necessary.

Serve the dip with some of the dukkah sprinkled over alongside vegetable crisps/chips. To eat, dunk the crisps into the dip and then back into the remaining dukkah, which will cling to the wet dip.

ROASTED RED PEPPER RAITA

Serve this colourful, cooling dip as part of a summer spread. A spicy lentil crisp/chip or cracker works well as a dipper here.

2 red (bell) peppers

1 tsp balsamic vinegar

1 tsp olive oil

pinch of salt

400 g/14 oz. Greek/US strained plain yogurt

seeds of ½ a pomegranate

1 tsp sumac

spicy lentil crisps/chips or crackers, to serve

SERVES 4–6

Grill/broil or roast the red peppers until they're charred on all sides. Wrap in a plastic bag (which makes them easier to peel afterwards), set aside to cool, then peel, deseed and chop into short strips.

Put the pepper strips in a bowl, add the balsamic vinegar, olive oil and salt and mix together. Set a few of the pepper strips aside. Fold through the yogurt and stir in most of the pomegranate seeds, setting aside 1 tablespoon to use as garnish. Stir in ½ teaspoon of the sumac.

Just before serving, garnish the raita with the reserved pepper strips and pomegranate seeds, and sprinkle over the remaining sumac.

MARINATED FETA DIP

You'll need to make this at least a day ahead. You can pop whatever you like in the oil – from chillies/chiles to pink peppercorns. Make sure you serve tortilla chips or chunks of bread to spoon the cheese onto.

400 g/14 oz. feta cheese, cut into small chunks

400 ml/1¾ cups good-quality olive oil

grated zest of 1 lemon

1 tbsp fennel seeds

1 red onion, thinly sliced

3 fresh thyme or rosemary sprigs

Homemade Tortilla Chips (see page 118) or chunks of bread, to serve

SERVES 4

Put all the ingredients in a sterilized jar and pop it in the refrigerator for a few days. If you only have a night, warm the oil with everything except the cheese in a pan. Let it cool, then add the cheese and refrigerate, until you are ready to serve.

Serve with a spoon to remove the feta from the oil and tortilla chips or chunks of bread for dipping.

WHIPPED BLUE CHEESE DIP

This recipe is for a lighter blue cheese dip made with yogurt. It is particularly delicious served with crunchy carrot batons.

150 g/scant ¾ cup Greek/US strained plain yogurt

150 ml/scant ¾ cup sour cream

90 g/generous ¾ cup blue cheese, such as Stilton or Gorgonzola

3 tbsp mayonnaise

pinch of salt

splash of lemon juice

1 tbsp chopped/snipped fresh chives, plus extra for decoration

carrot batons, to serve

SERVES 4–6

Place all of the ingredients except the chives in a food processor or blender, and blitz until smooth.

Transfer to a bowl and stir in the chives.

Sprinkle some extra chives on top for decoration. Serve with carrot batons.

DIP DECADENCE

Rich & luxurious dips for pure indulgence

RANCH DIP

Ranch dip is an all-American classic, perfect for serving at summer parties. It is rich and creamy and bursting with herbs.

60 ml/¼ cup buttermilk

150 g/5½ oz. cream cheese

40 ml/2½ tbsp mayonnaise

1 garlic clove, peeled and chopped

1 tbsp olive oil

juice of ½ lemon

1 tbsp chopped fresh chives

1 tbsp chopped fresh parsley

1 tbsp chopped fresh dill

½ tsp paprika

1 tsp Dijon mustard

salt and black pepper

Vegetable Crisps/Chips (see page 123), to serve

SERVES 6–8

In a bowl, whisk together the buttermilk, cream cheese and mayonnaise until smooth.

Put the garlic, olive oil, lemon juice, chives, parsley and dill in a food processor and blitz until very finely chopped and the oil has emulsified. Make sure that there are no large pieces of garlic.

Fold the herb oil into the cream cheese mixture with the paprika and mustard, mixing well so that it is all combined. Season with salt and pepper.

Spoon into a serving bowl and serve with the vegetable crisps/chips, if liked.

Variation

Cheddar, Bacon & Onion Ranch Dip Fry or sauté 4 rashers/slices of lean bacon until crisp and chop into small pieces. Allow to cool and stir into the dip (omitting the dill from the original recipe), along with 4 tablespoons grated Cheddar cheese. Garnish with a handful of chopped spring onions/scallions and serve with giant pretzels for dipping.

FRENCH ONION DIP

When onions are roasted, they develop a sweet caramel flavour, perfect for this dip, which is something of a retro classic. Here it is served with deliciously light and crunchy potato crisps/chips.

4 onions

5 sprigs of fresh thyme

2 tbsp olive oil

250 g/9 oz. cream cheese, at room temperature

3 tbsp crème fraîche

salt and black pepper

Classic Potato Crisps/Chips (see page 122) or other favourite crackers, to serve

SERVES 6

Preheat the oven to 180°C (350°F) Gas 4.

Peel the onions and cut them into quarters. Put the onions in a roasting pan, add the thyme sprigs and drizzle with the olive oil. Season well with salt and pepper and bake in the preheated oven for 30–40 minutes until the onions are soft and have started to caramelize. Give them a stir towards the end of cooking so they don't burn. Remove from the oven and leave to cool. Discard any onions that have gone black as they will add bitterness to the dip.

Remove the thyme sprigs and run your fingers along them to remove the leaves, reserving one sprig for garnish, if you wish. Add the leaves and onions in their cooking juices to a blender and blitz to a smooth purée.

Whisk the cream cheese into the crème fraîche and blend with the onion purée. Taste for seasoning, adding more salt and black pepper if needed.

Spoon the dip into a bowl and garnish with the reserved thyme leaves. Serve with potato crisps/chips or crackers.

BLUE CHEESE & WALNUT DIP

If you prefer a really strong blue cheese, replace the Gorgonzola Dolce with Stilton or another hard blue cheese and blitz in a blender with the sour cream until smooth.

100 g/3½ oz. walnut pieces or halves

1 tsp finely chopped fresh rosemary

½ tsp finely grated lemon zest

1 tbsp olive oil

1 tsp caster/granulated sugar

100 g/½ cup cream cheese

80 g/3 oz. Gorgonzola Dolce or other creamy blue cheese

60 ml/¼ cup sour cream

salt and black pepper

celery sticks/ribs, green apple wedges or breadsticks, to serve

SERVES 4–6

Preheat the oven to 180°C (350°F) Gas 4.

Put the walnuts, rosemary and lemon zest in a baking pan and drizzle with the olive oil. Sprinkle over the sugar and season with salt and pepper. Shake the pan so that all the nuts are coated in the oil and herbs. Bake in the preheated oven for about 5 minutes until the nuts are hot, taking care that they do not burn. Remove from the oven and leave to cool.

Blitz three-quarters of the walnuts in a food processor or blender. Tip the ground nuts into a bowl with the cream cheese, blue cheese and sour cream and whisk together until smooth and creamy with a slight nutty crunch. Season to taste. Spoon the dip into a bowl and sprinkle over the remaining roasted nuts.

Serve with celery sticks, apple wedges or breadsticks.

PEANUT SATAY DIP

Peanut satay makes a great dip to serve as a snack before a Thai meal with prawn/shrimp crackers and carrot batons to dip. This recipe uses solid creamed coconut, but you can substitute it for a small can of creamed coconut if you need to, though as it's runnier you may not need to add the crème fraîche.

1 tbsp soy or tamari sauce

1 tbsp soft dark brown sugar

100-g/3½-oz. block creamed coconut

2 tbsp crunchy peanut butter

150 g/5½ oz. cream cheese

juice of 1 lime

2 tbsp crème fraîche or sour cream

prawn/shrimp crackers and/or carrot batons, to serve

TO GARNISH

1 tbsp roasted peanuts, finely chopped

fresh coriander/cilantro leaves

SERVES 4–6

In a bowl, whisk the soy sauce and brown sugar together until the sugar has dissolved. Put the mixture in a blender with the creamed coconut, peanut butter, cream cheese and lime juice and blitz until smooth. Fold through the crème fraîche to loosen.

Spoon into a bowl and garnish with chopped peanuts and coriander leaves, if you like. Serve straight away with prawn crackers and/or carrot batons, for dipping.

(Note that if you chill the dip in the refrigerator it will set, so you will need to bring it to room temperature again or heat gently before serving.)

TRUFFLED CAULIFLOWER DIP

Cauliflower is a hugely versatile and often underrated vegetable. Roasting gives it a delicious nuttiness that balances well here with the richness of truffle oil to make a velvety and indulgent dip.

½ a head of cauliflower, chopped into 1-cm/⅜-inch pieces

vegetable oil, for drizzling

3 tbsp double/heavy cream or dairy-free substitute if preferred

1 tsp truffle oil

salt

6–8 slices thinly sliced toasted sourdough bread, to serve

SERVES 4

Preheat the oven to 180°C (350°F) Gas 4.

Put the cauliflower in a saucepan, cover with water and set over a low-medium heat. Simmer for about 5 minutes, then drain and scatter onto a baking sheet. Drizzle the cauliflower with a little vegetable oil and sprinkle with salt. Roast in the oven for 10–12 minutes until just starting to turn golden.

Remove from the oven and return to the saucepan. Add the cream and a pinch of salt. Purée using a hand-held electric/stick blender (or in a blender) until it resembles cottage cheese. Set aside to cool, then put in the refrigerator.

Once the dip has chilled completely, stir in the truffle oil. Serve at room temperature with toasted bread.

MEDITERRANEAN TOMATO HUMMUS

1 garlic bulb (unpeeled)

coarse sea salt and 1 tsp olive oil, for baking the garlic

10 sun-dried tomato halves

320 g/2 cups cooked chickpeas/garbanzo beans, plus 60 ml/¼ cup of the cooking liquid, or more if needed

1 tbsp tahini

2 tbsp extra virgin olive oil (plus extra to serve)

1 bunch of fresh basil, chopped, plus a few whole leaves to garnish

1 sprig of fresh thyme, leaves only

3 tbsp chopped fresh parsley leaves

2 tsp lemon juice

½ tsp salt, or to taste

¼ tsp dried rosemary

black pepper

SERVES 2–3

With roasted garlic, sun-dried tomatoes and fresh herbs, this aromatic hummus is packed full of Mediterranean ingredients.

Preheat the oven to 180°C (350°F) Gas 4.

Brush the garlic bulb with oil, rub in some coarse sea salt, wrap in foil and bake in the preheated oven for 40 minutes or until the garlic flesh becomes soft.

Soak the sun-dried tomatoes in warm water for about 30 minutes. Drain and discard the water. (If using oil-packed tomato halves, there's no need to soak them, but omit 2 tablespoons of olive oil in the recipe, as the tomatoes will bring enough oil to the hummus.) Chop.

Blend the chickpeas with the tahini, slowly adding the cooking liquid, until it has reached the desired consistency.

Spoon the hummus out into a bigger bowl and stir in the chopped tomato halves, half the garlic bulb paste (save the other half to add to other dishes), the olive oil, chopped basil, thyme leaves, 2 tablespoons of the chopped parsley, the lemon juice, salt and freshly ground black pepper to taste. Sprinkle with the dried rosemary and the remaining chopped parsley, and garnish with the basil leaves and a drizzle of olive oil before serving.

CASHEW & ROASTED TOMATO DIP

This dip has a wonderful nutty texture and the roasted tomatoes give it a sweet, smoky taste.

200 g/7 oz. unsalted cashew nuts, soaked in a bowl of water overnight

250 g/9 oz. sweet cherry tomatoes

1 tbsp olive oil, plus extra to serve

1 tbsp balsamic glaze or good-quality balsamic vinegar

1 tsp caster/granulated sugar

2 large sprigs of fresh thyme

200 ml/7 fl. oz. buttermilk

juice of 1 lemon, plus extra to taste

salt and black pepper

Paprika Pitta Chips (see page 118) or crusty bread, to serve

SERVES 4

Preheat the oven to 140°C (275°F) Gas 1.

Cut the tomatoes in half and put, cut-side up, in a roasting pan. Drizzle with the olive oil and balsamic and season well with salt and pepper. Sprinkle over the sugar. Pull the thyme sprigs between your fingers to remove the tiny leaves and sprinkle the leaves over the tomatoes. Roast the tomatoes in the preheated oven for about 1½–2 hours, until almost dried but still a little soft. Remove from the oven and leave to cool.

Drain the cashews and discard the water. Put the nuts in a blender with the buttermilk, lemon juice and most of the roasted tomatoes, along with their juices. Reserve a few tomatoes for garnish.

Blitz to a smooth purée and taste for seasoning, adding salt, pepper or lemon juice to taste. Spoon into a bowl and top with the reserved roasted tomatoes and a drizzle of olive oil. Serve with paprika pitta chips or slices of crusty bread for dipping.

MONT D'OR DIP

Mont d'Or, or Vacherin Mont d'Or, is a cow's milk cheese from Switzerland, named after the mountain itself. Wrapped traditionally in a spruce box to help contain the flavours within, it is one of the world's most celebrated cheeses. Part of the reason for this is that it is only produced in winter, meaning availability is limited. Eaten *au naturel*, you cut away the top rind and scoop out the unctuous centre. Baked whole in its box, the cheese melts to a gooey, almost liquid perfection and is best served with breadsticks or potato crisps/chips.

1 small Mont d'Or cheese, 490 g/ 1 lb. 2 oz., at room temperature

2 garlic cloves, thinly sliced

2 sprigs of fresh rosemary, leaves picked

60 ml/4 tbsp Jura wine or dry fino sherry

drizzle of extra virgin olive oil

black pepper

Grissini (see page 121) and/or potato crisps/chips, to serve

SERVES 4–6

Preheat the oven to 200°C (400°F) Gas 6 and line a baking pan with baking paper.

Discard the wooden lid from the Mont d'Or box. Make lots of small cuts in the top of the cheese and carefully poke in the garlic slices and rosemary leaves. Pour the wine and olive oil over the cheese and season with pepper. Place in the prepared pan and bake for about 25–30 minutes or until the cheese is molten, bubbling and lightly golden.

Stir the melted cheese mixture until smooth, then transfer to a platter and serve with grissini and/or potato crisps/chips for dipping.

DU HAUT-DOUBS
DOUBS PAR FROMAGERIE DES FOURGS - 25300

DIP IT LIKE IT'S HOT

Warm dips for cold nights

MARYLAND CRAB DIP

A rich and creamy dip with mild, spicy heat. For a twist, fold in chopped lobster or prawns/shrimp in place of the crab.

150 g/5½ oz. cream cheese

125 ml/½ cup buttermilk

2 tbsp mayonnaise

1 tbsp hot chilli sauce (such as Frank's)

juice of 1 lemon

120 g/4½ oz. Cheddar cheese or provolone, grated

100 g/3½ oz. white or brown crab meat

pinch of chilli/chili powder

3 tbsp panko breadcrumbs

black pepper

celery sticks, to serve

SERVES 6–8

Preheat the oven to 180°C (350°F) Gas 4.

Place the cream cheese, buttermilk and mayonnaise in a bowl and whisk together until smooth. Add the hot sauce, a grind of black pepper and the lemon juice, and whisk to combine.

Divide the grated cheese into two-thirds and one-third. Add the larger portion to the cream cheese mixture along with the crab meat and chilli powder, and fold together gently until mixed. Spoon into an ovenproof bowl. Cover the top with the remaining cheese and sprinkle over the panko breadcrumbs.

Bake in the preheated oven for 20–25 minutes until the cheese on top is golden brown. Remove from the oven and leave to cool for 10 minutes before serving with celery sticks for dipping.

WARM OLIVE & ARTICHOKE DIP

This is a really savoury and moreish dip with a kick of saltiness from both the olives and Parmesan. Use black olives in place of the green ones, if you prefer them.

160 g/5½ oz. stoned/pitted green olives (drained weight), rinsed to remove excess brine

290 g/10 oz. chargrilled artichokes preserved in olive oil, drained

1 tbsp Worcestershire sauce

1 tsp wholegrain mustard

150 ml/5 fl. oz. cup crème fraîche or sour cream

150 g/5½ oz. cream cheese

50 g/2 oz. Parmesan cheese, finely grated

black pepper

warm crusty bread, to serve

SERVES 6

Preheat the oven to 180°C (350°F) Gas 4.

Put the drained olives and artichokes in a food processor or blender and blitz until chopped into small pieces.

In a mixing bowl, whisk together the Worcestershire sauce, mustard, crème fraîche and cream cheese until smooth. Reserve a few tablespoons of the grated Parmesan and stir the rest into the mixture. Fold in the chopped artichokes and olives and mix well until everything is coated with the cream cheese mixture. Taste for seasoning – you shouldn't need to add any salt but add black pepper as required.

Spoon into an ovenproof dish and spread out in an even layer. Sprinkle the reserved Parmesan over the top and bake in the preheated oven for 25–30 minutes until the Parmesan starts to turn golden on top. Remove from the oven and leave to cool slightly before serving.

Serve spread onto warm crusty bread.

HOT BUTTERED CRAB DIP

Brown crab meat often gets overlooked in favour of fresher-tasting white meat, but it has an incredible richness which makes it a great base for bisques and dips. And it LOVES Amontillado sherry.

2 tbsp Amontillado sherry

75 g/⅓ cup unsalted butter, cut into cubes

450 g/1 lb. brown crab meat

2 tbsp grated Parmesan cheese

good pinch of mace

cayenne pepper, to taste

squeeze of fresh lemon juice

toast fingers or pitta chips, to serve

SERVES 4

Measure the sherry into a pan and add the cubed butter. Gently melt over a low heat, then stir in the crab meat and Parmesan. Heat through to just under boiling point and simmer for a couple of minutes, then take off the heat and season to taste with mace (go easy, it's powerful), cayenne pepper and a squeeze of lemon. (You probably won't need salt.)

Pour into warmed ramekin dishes, sprinkle lightly with a little more cayenne pepper and serve with toast fingers or pitta chips.

BLUE CHEESE FONDUE DIP

This fondue dip is perfect served as an appetizer with grissini, grapes and asparagus. Alternatively, try serving it as a dessert course with ripe pears, cut into quarters for dipping.

125 ml/½ cup sweet white wine, such as German Riesling or Gewürztraminer, plus an extra 1 tbsp

400 g/14 oz. creamy blue cheese, such as Gorgonzola or Roquefort, coarsely chopped

1 tsp cornflour/cornstarch, mixed with 1 tbsp of the wine

TO SERVE

Grissini (see page 121)

black grapes

asparagus spears, lightly cooked

SERVES 6

To prepare the fondue, pour the wine into the fondue pot and heat until simmering on the stovetop.

Gradually stir in the blue cheese, then the cornflour mixture, stirring constantly until smooth.

Transfer the pot to its tabletop burner and serve with grissini, grapes and asparagus.

HOT PHILLY STEAK DIP

This recipe is inspired by one of the most popular steak recipes in America, the Philly cheesesteak – a steak sandwich made with thin slices of beef, topped with melting cheese. Dip in tortilla chips or crusty bread while watching the Super Bowl.

1 green (bell) pepper

1 onion

1 tbsp olive oil

1 tsp balsamic glaze or vinegar

1 tsp caster/granulated sugar

6 slices roast beef

250 g/9 oz. cream cheese

125 ml/½ cup ranch salad dressing

1 tbsp creamed horseradish

100 g/3½ oz. provolone or Cheddar cheese, grated

salt and black pepper

Homemade Tortilla Chips (see page 118) or crusty bread, to serve

SERVES 6–8

Preheat the oven to 180°C (350°F) Gas 4.

Cut away the top of the green pepper and discard. Cut the pepper in half, remove all of the seeds, then cut into small chunks about 1-cm/½-inch diameter. Peel and finely chop the onion. Put the peppers and onion in a large frying pan/skillet with the olive oil and fry over a gentle heat until the onions and peppers are soft and the onion starts to caramelize. Drizzle with the balsamic, sprinkle over the sugar, season with salt and pepper and fry/sauté for a few more minutes.

Cut the roast beef into small pieces and add to the pan. Cook for a minute or so, for the meat to absorb the flavours from the pan. Remove from the heat and leave to cool for a few minutes.

In a mixing bowl, whisk together the cream cheese, ranch dressing and creamed horseradish. Fold the grated cheese into the mixture with the beef and vegetables.

Bake in the preheated oven for about 20–25 minutes until the cheese has melted and the top of the dip has started to turn golden. Cool for 10 minutes before serving, as the dip should be served warm and not hot. Serve with tortilla chips or crusty bread for dipping.

Variation

Spicy Hot Philly Dip For a spicy version, fold in some finely chopped jarred jalapeños with the beef before baking.

HAWAIIAN-STYLE BACON & PINEAPPLE DIP

This decadent hot dip is made with gooey melted cheese, pineapple and salty pancetta. You can replace the pancetta with ready-cooked ham or fried bacon lardons if you prefer. Fresh pineapple is usually best as it has more flavour, but canned pineapple is also fine to use and is quicker to prepare.

100 g/3½ oz. pancetta rashers/slices

4 slices of fresh pineapple or 4 canned pineapple rings

250 g/9 oz. cream cheese

125 ml/½ cup Thousand Island dressing

1 tbsp sun-dried tomato purée/paste

100 g/3½ oz. Red Leicester | or Colby cheese, grated

salt and black pepper

Homemade Tortilla Chips (see page 118) or crusty bread, to serve

SERVES 6–8

Preheat the oven to 180°C (350°F) Gas 4.

Chop the pancetta into about 3-cm/1-inch pieces and put in a roasting pan.

If using a fresh pineapple, remove the skin, eyes and hard core, then chop into small pieces. If using canned pineapple, chop the rings into small pieces. Add the pineapple to the roasting pan and bake in the hot oven for 10 minutes. Remove from the oven and leave to cool slightly.

Put the cream cheese in a mixing bowl. Add the Thousand Island dressing and tomato purée and whisk together until smooth. Stir in the grated cheese, cooled pancetta and pineapple pieces, and season with salt and pepper. Bake in the preheated oven for 20–25 minutes until golden brown on top. Leave to cool slightly for about 10 minutes, then serve warm with tortilla chips or crusty bread for dipping.

Variation

Hawaiian 'Pizza' Dip Try using pepperoni slices instead of the pancetta and arrange them on top of the dip as you would with a pizza. To reinforce the theme, you can serve it with a pizza dough base, cut into wedges for dipping.

SPICY CHILLI BEAN DIP

Shiny, kidney-shaped black beans are especially popular in Latin American cooking. They are left whole in this recipe, but you could roughly mash after cooking to make the dip more gooey.

440 g/2 cups dried black beans

2 tbsp olive oil

1 red onion, chopped

4 garlic cloves, chopped

1 red (bell) pepper, deseeded and diced

1 tbsp ground cumin

2 tsp dried Greek oregano

2 tsp chilli/chili powder

2 x 400-g/14-oz. cans chopped tomatoes

TO SERVE

handful of fresh coriander/ cilantro leaves, chopped

Greek/US strained plain yogurt

warmed corn chips

SERVES 6–8

Put the dried beans in a saucepan with 2 litres/quarts cold water. Bring to the boil, then reduce the heat to a low simmer and cook the beans, uncovered, for about 1½ hours, until just tender and not falling apart. Drain well and set aside.

Heat the oil in a large, heavy-based saucepan set over a medium heat. When the oil is hot, add the onion, garlic and pepper and cook for 8–10 minutes, until softened. Stir in the cumin, oregano and chilli powder and fry for 1 minute.

Increase the heat to high. Add the tomatoes, beans and 250 ml/1 cup cold water and bring to the boil. Reduce the heat to low, partially cover the pan and cook for 1½–2 hours, adding a little more water from time to time if the mixture is drying or catching on the bottom of the pan.

Transfer the dip to a serving bowl and serve with the yogurt and coriander leaves on top and corn chips for dipping.

HOT BUFFALO CHICKEN WING DIP

This dip has the taste of hot buffalo wings but without the bother of getting messy fingers eating actual wings. Hot chilli sauces vary in strength, so add gradually and taste to ensure you don't end up with a dip that is too hot.

300 g/10½ oz. cream cheese

170 ml/¾ cup ranch salad dressing

125 ml/½ cup red hot chilli sauce (such as Frank's)

150 g/5½ oz. Cheddar cheese, grated

200 g/7 oz. cooked chicken breast

black pepper

Homemade Tortilla Chips (see page 118), to serve

SERVES 6–8

Preheat the oven to 180°C (350°F) Gas 4.

Put the cream cheese, ranch dressing and hot sauce in a bowl and whisk together until smooth. Stir in the cheese. Remove any skin from the chicken breasts and discard, then chop into small pieces and stir into the sauce. Season with ground black pepper and taste. You can add a little salt if you wish, but there should be sufficient salt from the dressing and hot sauce.

Bake in the preheated oven for 25–30 minutes until the top of the dip starts to turn light golden brown. Remove from the oven and leave to cool for a short while, then serve warm with tortilla chips.

Variation

Vegetarian Buffalo 'Chicken Wing' Dip To make a version suitable for vegetarians to enjoy, simply use a vegetarian cheese and replace the cooked chicken breast with butter/lima beans or small florets of steamed or boiled cauliflower.

TUNA MELT DIP

The tried-and-tested combination of tuna and melted Cheddar creates a hot dip that's sure to become a family favourite.

225 g/8 oz. cream cheese

2 tbsp butter, softened

2 tbsp mayonnaise

65 ml/½ cup sour cream

2 tbsp lemon juice

1–2 tbsp very finely diced spring onions/scallions

2 tbsp chopped fresh flat-leaf parsley

½ tsp paprika

¼ tsp ground black pepper

2 x 400-g/14 oz. cans tuna, drained

50 g/½ cup grated Cheddar cheese

Classic Potato Crisps/Chips (see page 122), to serve

SERVES 6–8

Preheat the oven to 180°C (350°F) Gas 4.

Blend the cream cheese with the softened butter. Add in the mayonnaise and sour cream and blend until smooth. Add the lemon juice, spring onion, parsley, paprika and pepper. Stir in the flaked, well-drained tuna and cheese.

Bake in the preheated oven for 10–15 minutes, until hot and bubbly. Remove from the oven and leave to cool for 10 minutes before serving with potato crisps/chips.

FONDUTA

If you don't have a truffle to hand for this creamy warm dip, a sprinkling of truffle oil will give a hint of the prized fragrance.

½ tsp cornflour/cornstarch

250 ml/1 cup milk

400 g/14 oz. Fontina cheese, chopped

35 g/2¼ tbsp unsalted butter, melted

4 egg yolks

freshly ground white pepper

1 white truffle (optional) or truffle oil

TO SERVE

steamed spring vegetables such as baby carrots, baby leeks, baby turnips, asparagus, fennel and mangetout, cut into bite-sized pieces if necessary

cubes of fresh bread

SERVES 6

Put the cornflour into a small bowl, add 1 tablespoon of the milk and stir until dissolved – this is called 'slaking'.

Put the remaining milk into the top section of a double boiler, then add the cheese and slaked cornflour. Place over a saucepan of simmering water and heat, stirring constantly, until the cheese has melted. Stir in the butter and remove from the heat.

Put the egg yolks into a bowl and whisk lightly. Whisk in a few tablespoons of the hot cheese mixture to warm the yolks. Pour this mixture back into the double boiler, stirring vigorously. Return the pan to the heat. Continue stirring until the mixture thickens.

To serve, ladle the cheese mixture into warmed bowls and sprinkle with freshly ground white pepper and shavings of truffle, if using. Alternatively, sprinkle with a few drops of truffle oil. Serve the bowls surrounded by the prepared vegetables and cubes of fresh bread for dipping.

DIP, DIP, HOORAY

Party dips to feed a crowd

BUTTER BEAN WHIP & CRUDITÉS PLATTER

400-g/14-oz. can butter/lima beans, drained

2 tbsp olive oil

1 tsp sea salt, or to taste

1 garlic clove, crushed

juice of 1 lemon

black pepper

vegetable crudités and/or crackers, to serve

TOPPING

2 tbsp olive oil

2 fresh rosemary sprigs, leaves picked

8 fresh sage leaves

2 fresh tarragon sprigs, leaves picked

2 spring onions/scallions, finely sliced

2 tsp capers, drained

grated zest of 1 lemon

SERVES 4

Perfect for your vegan and vegetarian guests and all lovers of vegetables. The butter/lima bean whip, with its citrus and garlic mix, is topped with sautéed spring onions/scallions, herbs and capers, and is a taste sensation.

For the dip, using a food processor or hand-held electric/stick blender, blend the beans, oil, ½ teaspoon salt, garlic, lemon juice and pepper. Taste and add the remaining salt if necessary.

For the topping, heat the oil in a sauté pan over a medium heat. Carefully add the herbs, spring onions and capers to the hot oil and fry for 1–2 minutes until crisp. Use a slotted spoon to carefully transfer the fried topping to paper towels to drain off any excess oil, reserving the oil in the pan.

To assemble, use a spatula or the back of a spoon to spread the bean dip over a nice plate or bowl. Top with the crispy herbs and a few splashes of the infused pan oil. Sprinkle over the lemon zest and serve with crudités and/or crackers.

SPICY BEER MUSTARD DIP
WITH MINI MAPLE-GLAZED SAUSAGES

80 g/3 oz. yellow mustard seeds

25 g/1 oz. black mustard seeds

125 ml/½ cup strong beer

125 ml/½ cup cider vinegar

80 g/½ cup soft dark brown sugar

40 ml/2½ tbsp maple syrup

1 tsp ground allspice

1 tbsp creamed horseradish

salt and black pepper

MAPLE-GLAZED SAUSAGES

24 mini sausages or 12 chipolatas

12 rashers/slices streaky bacon

a little olive oil

3 tbsp maple syrup

1 tbsp sesame seeds

SERVES 6–8

This delicious mustard dip is classically served with soft pretzels or sausages. Here it's paired with little cocktail sausages, which are the ideal size for dipping! Making your own mustard is easy, although you will need to soak the mustard seeds overnight.

Put the yellow and black mustard seeds in a bowl and pour over the beer and cider vinegar. Cover the bowl with clingfilm/plastic wrap and put in the refrigerator overnight to soak. The mustard seeds will absorb some of the liquid and become soft.

The following day, put the soaked seeds and soaking liquor into a food processor or blender with the sugar, maple syrup, ground allspice and creamed horseradish and blitz for a few minutes until smooth. It will still have some small pieces of mustard seed which give a great texture to the dip. Season with salt and pepper to your taste. This recipe makes plenty of mustard, so you may want to reserve half in a sealed jar and keep it in the refrigerator.

Preheat the oven to 180°C (350°F) Gas 4.

If using chipolatas, twist the centre of each sausage then cut with scissors to make 24 mini sausages. Cut

the bacon strips in half, wrap one half strip around each mini sausage and secure in place with a cocktail stick/toothpick. Put in a roasting pan and drizzle with a little olive oil and roast in the oven for about 25–30 minutes until the sausages turn golden brown. Drizzle with the maple syrup, sprinkle with the sesame seeds and bake for a further 5 minutes. Serve the sausages hot or cold with the spicy beer mustard dip.

LAYERED 'NACHO' DIP

One of the all-time favourite sharing plates is nachos – tortilla chips are served piled high with tomato salsa, guacamole, sour cream and grated cheese, then warmed under a grill/broiler. This dip version is layered up in a bowl and then warmed, ready to scoop out with crunchy tortilla chips.

Guacamole (see page 15)

Tomato Salsa (see page 15)

200 ml/7 fl. oz. sour cream

125 g/4½ oz. strong cheese, such as mature/sharp Cheddar, grated

handful of jarred jalapeño slices (optional)

Homemade Tortilla Chips (see page 118), to serve

SERVES 6

To assemble the dip, spoon the guacamole into a shallow serving bowl and spread out in a thick layer. Top with the tomato salsa, then spoon over the sour cream, scatter over the grated cheese and finish with jalapeños, if using.

Gently warm under a preheated grill/broiler just until the cheese starts to melt. Serve straight away with the tortilla chips.

SPICY RÉMOULADE DIP WITH SOUTHERN-STYLE CRAB FRITTERS

These Deep South-style crab fritters are perfect for sharing. Just make sure you make enough of the spicy rémoulade dip to go around!

250 ml/1 cup mayonnaise

1 tbsp Dijon mustard

1 tbsp tomato ketchup

1 garlic clove, crushed

1 tbsp paprika

1 tsp hot sauce, such as Tabasco

2 tbsp capers, coarsely chopped

small squeeze of fresh lemon juice

¼ tsp salt

SOUTHERN-STYLE CRAB FRITTERS

2 x 145-g/5¼-oz. cans lump crab meat

1 tbsp capers, coarsely chopped

a few fresh dill and flat-leaf parsley sprigs, chopped

1 tsp Worcestershire sauce

pinch of salt

1 egg

150 g/3 cups fresh breadcrumbs

vegetable oil, for shallow frying

SERVES 4–6 (MAKES 12 FRITTERS)

Start by making the dip; mix all the ingredients together and taste, adding a little more of any of the ingredients to your taste. Set aside.

To make the fritters, place the crab meat in a sieve/strainer and gently push down to extract the excess liquid, then leave to drain.

Place the capers, herbs, Worcestershire sauce, salt and egg in a mixing bowl, add 4 tablespoons of the spicy rémoulade sauce and whisk together, ensuring the egg is all fully incorporated. Fold in one-third of the breadcrumbs and all the crab meat, trying not to over-mix.

Place the remaining breadcrumbs in a flat dish. Take a ping-pong ball-sized portion of the crab mixture, roll into a ball between the palms of your hands and then flatten a little (the mixture will be slightly wet which is perfect for coating in the remaining breadcrumbs). Roll the ball in the breadcrumbs, coating it on all sides. Repeat with the remaining mixture to make 12 fritters.

Heat enough vegetable oil to coat the bottom of a saucepan. Fry the fritters for 2–4 minutes on each side until golden (you may need to cook them in batches to avoid over-crowding the pan). Remove from the pan and set on paper towels to drain. Season with a pinch of salt and transfer to a serving dish with the remaining spicy rémoulade dip on the side.

BLUE CHEESE, GARLIC & THYME DIP
WITH POTATO FRIES & PICKLED RED ONION RINGS

Blue cheese with fries is an all-time delicious combination, and the pickled red onion rings add just the right amount of acidity to cut through the richness. For this recipe it's best to use a mild blue cheese such as the blended cheese Cambozola, a Danish blue or Gorgonzola.

250 g/9 oz. Cambozola, diced

200 g/7 oz. Gruyère, grated

1 tbsp white vinegar

1 tbsp cornflour/cornstarch

1 tbsp olive oil

1 garlic clove, crushed

1 tsp chopped fresh thyme

150 ml/⅔ cup light blonde beer

3 tbsp single/light cream

salt and black pepper

PICKLED RED ONION RINGS

125 ml/½ cup cider vinegar

30 g/2½ tbsp granulated sugar

1 tsp salt

1 red onion, thinly sliced

1 garlic clove, thinly sliced

pinch of black peppercorns

POTATO FRIES

1 kg/2 lb. 4 oz. Maris Piper, Yukon Gold or King Edward potatoes

1 tbsp olive oil

SERVES 6

First make the pickled onion rings. Place the vinegar, 125 ml/½ cup water, the sugar and salt in a small saucepan and bring to the boil over a low heat. Let it boil for 1 minute, then remove from the heat.

Meanwhile, place the onion, garlic and peppercorns into a sterilized 350-ml/12-oz. jar. Pour the hot pickling mixture directly over the onion and seal the jar with a vinegar-safe lid. Cool and set aside until required.

Preheat the oven to 200°C (400°F) Gas 6 and line a large baking sheet with baking paper.

Cut the potatoes into thin fries, no more than 5 mm/¼ inch thick and place on the prepared baking sheet. Add the oil, salt and pepper and stir well. Bake in the oven for 45–50 minutes, stirring from time to time, until crisp and golden.

Meanwhile, combine the cheeses with a little pepper. Stir the vinegar and cornflour together until smooth. About 10 minutes before the potatoes are cooked, heat the oil in a fondue pot on the stovetop and gently fry the garlic and thyme over a low heat for 3 minutes until softened. Add the beer and cream and bring to the boil, then stir in the cheese until melted. Stir in the cornflour and vinegar mixture and simmer for about 1–2 minutes until it has thickened.

Arrange the potato fries on plates or in bowls and serve with the dip and pickled onion rings.

ROAST GARLIC HERBED LABNEH

Making labneh (also labne, labni or yogurt cheese) is very simple, but do bear in mind that it takes 24 hours to strain the yogurt. Serve this Middle Eastern cheese dip with hot pitta bread or vegetable crudités.

450 g/2 cups full-fat goat's milk yogurt

2 roast garlic cloves (see page 40)

grated zest of 1 lemon

3 tbsp finely chopped fresh flat-leaf parsley

1 tsp finely chopped fresh chives

1 tsp fresh thyme leaves

salt

TO SERVE

olive oil

pistachio nuts, finely ground

warm pitta bread or vegetable crudités

muslin/cheesecloth square and string

SERVES 4–6

First, make the labneh. Season the yogurt with salt to taste, mixing it in well. Put the yogurt in the centre of the muslin/cheesecloth square, fold up the muslin around the yogurt and tie tightly, forming a parcel. Suspend the muslin parcel over a deep, large bowl by tying it with string to a wooden spoon laid across the top of the bowl. Leave in the refrigerator for 24 hours, during which time the excess moisture will drip out of the parcel.

Squeeze the roast garlic out of the papery skin and mash into a paste. Flavour the labneh by mixing it with the roast garlic, lemon zest, parsley, chives and thyme.

Transfer the labneh to a dish. Use the back of a spoon to make a little hollow in the middle of the labneh, pour in a little olive oil, sprinkle with ground pistachio nuts and serve with hot pitta bread or vegetable crudités.

SCORCHED AUBERGINE & CAULIFLOWER DIP WITH ONION & POMEGRANATE SALAD

This is one of those moreish combinations you'll dream about for days. The dip is smoky, creamy and delicious with the sweet and tart onions.

2 large aubergines/eggplants (about 650 g/1 lb. 7 oz.)

½ cauliflower, cut into florets (about 200 g/7 oz.)

4 garlic cloves, unpeeled

1 tsp smoked cumin

4 tbsp extra virgin olive oil

juice of 1 lemon

2 tbsp tahini

1 tbsp each freshly chopped mint and flat-leaf parsley

1 tbsp pomegranate seeds

½ tsp sumac

salt and black pepper

purple basil, to garnish (optional)

SALAD

3 red onions

2 tbsp vegetable oil

4 tbsp pomegranate molasses

1 tsp maple syrup (optional)

2 tsp sumac

1 tsp sea salt flakes

2 wooden skewers, soaked for 30 minutes

SERVES 4

Preheat the oven to 200°C (400°F) Gas 6.

Blacken the aubergines over a gas hob/ring or barbecue/outdoor grill, turning regularly, until completely charred and collapsed. Allow to cool.

Place the cauliflower and garlic on a lined baking sheet and sprinkle with the cumin. Drizzle with 2 tablespoons of the olive oil and season. Bake in the preheated oven for 10 minutes, then turn and cook for another 10 minutes or until tender and the cauliflower has coloured. Squeeze the garlic out of the skins and set aside with the cauliflower to cool.

Slit the aubergines lengthways and scoop out the flesh, discarding the skins. Leave in a sieve/strainer to drain for 30 minutes.

In a serving bowl, stir the lemon juice and 3 tablespoons water into the tahini until it loosens. Add the mint and flat-leaf parsley and season. Mash the aubergines, garlic and cauliflower with a fork (reserving a few cauli florets for garnish), then stir them into the tahini mixture. Top with the reserved florets, pomegranate seeds, sumac and purple basil, if liked. Pour the remaining oil around the edge.

For the salad, peel and quarter the onions, leaving the roots and tips on. Toss the onions in the oil and skewer them. Fry in a very hot griddle/grill pan until charred.

Drizzle the hot onions with the molasses and maple syrup, (if using), sprinkle with the sumac and salt flakes. Serve.

ROMESCO DIP WITH GRILLED SPRING ONIONS

Romesco is a Spanish dip made with (bell) peppers, almonds, bread and garlic that is traditionally eaten with the first onions of spring.

6 tomatoes, halved

4 red (bell) peppers, halved and deseeded

8 tbsp olive oil

50 g/generous ⅓ cup hazelnuts or almonds, blanched

15-cm/6-inch piece of stale white baguette/French bread, broken into chunks

3 garlic cloves, peeled

1 tbsp sherry vinegar

½ tsp smoked paprika

12 spring onions/scallions, tops and bottoms trimmed

salt and black pepper

SERVES 4–6

Preheat the oven to 200°C (400°F) Gas 6.

Put the tomatoes and peppers in separate roasting pans, season and drizzle 1 tablespoon of the olive oil over each. Roast in the preheated oven for about 35 minutes, or until the pepper skins have started to blacken.

Meanwhile, blitz the blanched nuts in a food processor or blender and leave them in there.

Remove the tomatoes from the pan and set aside. Add the chunks of baguette to the tomato juices in the pan. Let cool.

Remove the peppers from the pan, put into a bowl, cover with cling film/plastic wrap and allow to cool. Once cooled, remove and discard the pepper skins and add the flesh to the food processor, along with the tomatoes. Add 4 tablespoons of the olive oil, along with the garlic, soaked bread, sherry vinegar and smoked paprika. Blitz until smooth.

To prepare the spring onions, preheat the grill/broiler to high. Drizzle the remaining olive oil over them and toss to coat. Arrange them on the grill pan and cook, turning, for 3–5 minutes. Serve warm with the romesco dip.

CHIP, DIP, REPEAT

All the dippers & dunkers you could need

CHIA SEED RYE CRACKERS

You can either use these crackers for dipping after they've cooled down, or spread any dip you have over them, top that with veggies or other toppings of your choice and munch your worries away!

130 g/¾ cup rye flour

130 g/¾ cup unbleached plain/all-purpose flour

15 g/2 tbsp chia seeds

4 g/scant 1 tsp salt

black pepper, to taste

60 ml/¼ cup olive oil or light sesame oil

1 tsp dark agave or maple syrup

hummus, cucumber and micro cress, to serve (optional)

MAKES 12–16 CRACKERS

Combine all the dry ingredients in a large bowl.

Emulsify oil, agave or maple syrup with 60 ml/¼ cup water with a whisk, and then slowly add them to the flour and seed mixture, stirring until well combined. The dough should quickly form a ball and shouldn't be sticky. Knead a couple of times; just enough to make sure all the ingredients are evenly distributed. Wrap in cling film/plastic wrap and let sit at room temperature for 10 minutes. Resting the dough makes rolling it out much easier.

Preheat the oven to 200°C (400°F) Gas 6.

Divide the dough into three equal pieces. Roll out a very thin layer of dough between two sheets of baking parchment. If you like really crunchy crackers, the dough should be almost paper-thin, but if you like a bit of texture, roll to desired thickness.

Use a knife or pizza cutter to cut out shapes. Squares or rectangles are practical choices, since you'll have not much leftover dough. Transfer the crackers to a baking sheet lined with baking parchment using a thin spatula or a knife. Prick each a couple of times with a fork. Bake in the preheated oven for 4–7 minutes, depending on

the thickness of the crackers. Remember, they shouldn't brown, just get slightly golden. They will firm up as they cool, so don't expect them to be cracker-crunchy straight out of the oven.

Here, they are spread with hummus and topped with cucumber and micro cress, but you can eat them how you prefer! Store in an airtight container after they've cooled completely.

HOMEMADE TORTILLA CHIPS

pictured on pages 93 & 102

The ultimate dipper, perfect for serving with all manner of dips and snacks.

8 small soft wheat flour tortillas

sunflower or vegetable oil, for frying

SERVES 6

Stack the tortillas and cut each one into 8 even triangles, like a pizza.

Pour about 2.5 cm/1 inch of oil into a small pan, then put over a medium-high heat. When the oil is hot, you can test-fry one tortilla triangle – it should take about 30 seconds for the first side to become crisp. Using tongs or a slotted spoon, turn the tortilla over to fry the other side.

Fry the remaining tortillas in batches and, when golden brown, drain on paper towels.

When cool, store in an airtight container until ready to use.

PAPRIKA PITTA CHIPS

pictured on pages 18 & 72

A little added seasoning elevates these crispy chips and makes them a perfect partner for any creamy dips.

2 tbsp olive oil

1 tbsp smoked paprika

5 white pitta breads, halved lengthways and cut into strips

salt and black pepper

SERVES 4–6

Preheat the oven to 200°C (400°F) Gas 6.

Drizzle a foil-lined baking sheet with the olive oil, then sprinkle over the paprika and some salt and black pepper. Put the pitta bread strips on the baking sheet and mix to coat in the oil and seasoning.

Bake in the preheated oven for 8 minutes until slightly coloured and crisp.

BAGEL TOASTS

pictured on page 27

Bagel toasts work really well and are so simple to make; there's no comparison between shop-bought and homemade.

3 plain bagels, stale is fine!

3 tbsp olive oil

1 tbsp poppy seeds or sesame seeds (optional)

SERVES 4

Preheat the grill/broiler to hot.

Using a sharp knife, slice each bagel horizontally into 4 and arrange the thin slices on the grill pan.

Grill on one side until lightly browned, then remove from the oven and turn over. Brush the oil over the untoasted side of the bagels. Scatter over the seeds, if using, and return to the grill/broiler. Toast until crisp and golden.

Serve immediately or let cool and store in an airtight container for up to 2 days.

CROSTINI

pictured on page 38

Crispy crostini work wonderfully for dipping and also for topping with paté or spreads.

2 wholemeal/wholewheat baguettes/French sticks, each sliced into 30–35 slices about 5 mm/¼ inch thick

100 ml/½ cup olive oil

SERVES 4–6

Heat a griddle/grill pan over a high heat and brush each side of the bread with olive oil. Cook the bread slices, in batches, for 1 minute on each side, until they are toasted and crisp. Remove and put onto a wire rack to cool.

Alternatively, bake them on a baking sheet in an oven at 180°C (350°F) Gas 4 for about 8–10 minutes.

GRISSINI

Crunchy homemade grissini are delicious on their own, but pairing them with a tasty dip for a snack or an easy appetizer is a great idea.

140 ml /⅔ cup lukewarm water

5 g/scant 2 tsp active dry yeast

5 g/1 tsp barley malt or agave syrup

190 g/1½ cups unbleached plain/ all-purpose flour

60 g/½ cup wholemeal/ wholewheat flour

4 g/scant 1 tsp salt

2 tbsp raw, unhulled sesame seeds, plus 1 tbsp extra for sprinkling

3 tbsp light sesame or olive oil

MAKES 20 GRISSINI

In a bowl, combine the water with the yeast and malt. Whisk and let sit for 15 minutes. The yeast will start to foam lightly.

In a separate bowl, combine the flours, salt, sesame seeds and 2 tablespoons of the oil. Stir in the bubbly yeast mixture and knead until smooth, about 4 minutes. Place on a baking sheet lined with baking parchment. Use a silicone spatula to oil the dough lightly. Let rise in the oven with only the light on, for 1 hour.

Preheat the oven to 180°C (350°F) Gas 4.

Form the dough into an oval shape then cut into 1-cm/ ⅜-inch strips using a sharp wide knife. Stretch each strip with your fingers into a long grissino; some strips will be longer and thicker, so you'll be able to stretch two or three grissini out of them. From this amount of dough, you should get 20 grissini (35 cm/14 inches long and 1 cm/⅜ inch thick). They do puff a little while baking in the oven.

Place the stretched grissini on a second baking sheet lined with baking parchment, roughly 7 mm/¼ inch apart. Brush with the remaining oil and sprinkle with the extra sesame seeds. Bake in the preheated oven for 12–15 minutes in two batches, rotating them halfway through. Let cool and serve with any dip. If any are leftover, store in a sealable bag at room temperature.

CLASSIC POTATO CRISPS/CHIPS *pictured on page 63*

You can't beat a good homemade potato crisp/chip for dipping and snacking on. Feel free to add different seasonings to change things up too.

800 g/1¾ lb. small waxy fingerling potatoes, such as Anya, Pink Fir Apple or Kipfler, cut into 3-mm/⅛-inch thick slices

125 ml/½ cup olive oil

125 ml/½ cup vegetable oil

SERVES 6

Bring a large saucepan of lightly salted water to the boil. Add the sliced potatoes, cover the pan and remove from the heat. Leave in the hot water for 5 minutes.

Drain well and arrange the slices on a wire rack in a single layer until completely cool.

Put the oils in a saucepan or large frying pan/skillet set over a high heat. When the oil is hot, cook the potato slices in batches for 5–6 minutes each, turning once or twice, until crisp and golden.

Remove from the oil using a metal slotted spoon and drain on paper towels.

VEGETABLE CRISPS/CHIPS

pictured on page 114

These no-fry veggie crisps/chips require a little effort in the kitchen, but they are so much more special than your average shop-bought potato crisp. Made from highly nutritious root vegetables, they are bursting with earthy, complex flavours to take your dipping game to the next level. Do not expect them to be as crunchy as deep-fried crisps, but their amazingly rich taste will compensate for that.

400 g/3 large carrots

400 g/2 large beetroots/beets (you can use regular or a mix of golden or candied)

400 g/3 large parsnips

3 tbsp olive oil

1 tsp fine sea salt

dehydrator

SERVES 4–6

Scrub all the root vegetables well and remove the tops and any black spots. Using a mandoline, slice them lengthways to get the longest strips possible. Small pieces will shrink into bite-size crisps/chips. Also, the slices should not be see-through thin.

Place in separate bowls and add 1 tablespoon of oil and a pinch of salt to each batch. Mix thoroughly.

Place on dehydrator trays in a single layer and dehydrate for 2 hours on maximum temperature, then lower the temperature to 50°C (100°F) and dehydrate for another 5 hours, or until crispy.

HERBY BREADSTICKS

This long, crispy breadstick with the addition of mixed dried herbs is delightful served with hummus or a melted cheese fondue dip.

300 g/2¼ cups plain/all-purpose flour

2 tsp fast-action yeast

2 tsp salt

1 tsp sugar

4 tbsp/¼ cup olive oil

120–150 ml/½–⅔ cup lukewarm water

pinch of mixed dried herbs

pinch of cayenne pepper

salt and black pepper

SERVES 4–6

Preheat the oven to 170°C (325°F) Gas 3.

Combine the flour, yeast, salt and sugar in a bowl. Make a well in the centre, pour in the olive oil and water, and stir until well combined and the dough comes together. It should be soft but not sticky.

Knead the dough for 10 minutes by hand, cover with oiled cling film/plastic wrap or a damp cloth and leave it to rise in a warm place for 40–60 minutes, or until doubled in size.

Divide the dough in half and keep half wrapped up so that it does not dry out. Roll half the dough out into a flat rectangle about 5 mm–1 cm/¼–⅜ inch thick, then cut it into 1-cm/⅜-inch-wide strips. Roll the strips into pencil-width tubes. Repeat with the other half of the dough.

Spread the mixed dried herbs, cayenne pepper and salt and pepper on a board, then roll the breadsticks in them and put them on a floured baking sheet. Bake in the preheated oven for 20–30 minutes until golden.

Remove from the oven and let cool on a wire rack.

SEEDED AMARANTH CRACKERS

pictured on page 41

Adding amaranth flour gives crackers a little more substance.

45 g/⅓ cup amaranth flour

40 g/⅓ cup milled flaxseeds

40 g/¼ cup sunflower seeds

1 tsp sea salt

¼ tsp onion powder or ½ small chopped onion

20 g/⅛ cup pumpkin seeds

2 tbsp milled hemp seeds

1 tbsp melted coconut oil, plus extra for greasing

60 ml/¼ cup water

SERVES 4

Preheat the oven to 150°C (300°F) Gas 2. Grease a baking sheet with a thin layer of coconut oil.

Pulse all of the dry ingredients in a food processor – you can leave the seeds in a roughly chopped state, if you prefer more texture. Then add the coconut oil and water and blend again until all the ingredients come together into a dough.

Roll the dough thinly onto the prepared baking sheet and bake in the preheated oven for 45–50 minutes. Set aside to cool, then break into pieces. Store in an airtight container until ready to serve.

SQUID INK CRACKERS

pictured on page 13

These deluxe crackers will add a flair of class to any mezze dip selection.

300 g/2¼ cups plain/all-purpose flour

1 tsp baking powder

1 tsp salt

½ tsp cayenne pepper

80 ml/⅓ cup olive oil

3 x 4 g/⅙ oz. squid ink sachets

SERVES 4–6

Preheat the oven to 180°C (350°F) Gas 4.

Mix the flour, baking powder, salt and cayenne pepper in a large mixing bowl, and make a well in the middle. Mix 150 ml/⅔ cup water with the olive oil and squid ink, then add to the well. Stir gently, slowly incorporating the dry ingredients until a dough forms. Turn out the dough onto a floured surface, and knead for about 3–5 minutes, or until smooth. Divide the dough into 15 pieces and roll them into the desired shapes with a rolling pin.

Transfer the shapes to a baking sheet lined with baking parchment and bake in the preheated oven for about 10–15 minutes, or until crisp on the undersides. Cool on a wire rack. Keep in an airtight container for up to 3 days before serving.

Tip: Squid ink is available in convenient sachets from Mediterranean grocery stores.

INDEX

RECIPE CREDITS

Fiona Beckett
Hot Buttered Crab Dip

Jordan Bourke
Avocado Miso Dip
Dukkah

Chloe Coker & Jane Montgomery
Baba Ganoush
Herby Breadsticks
Paprika Pitta Chips

Ross Dobson
Muhammara
Spicy Chilli Bean Dip

Amy Ruth Finegold
Crostini
Flax-speckled Hummus
Light Aubergine Dip
Seeded Amaranth Crackers
Spiced Beetroot Dip
White Bean & Spinach Dip

Matt Follas
Truffled Cauliflower Dip

Ben Fordham & Felipe Fuentes Cruz
Guacamole
Tomato salsa

Dunja Gulin
Chia Seed Rye Crackers
Grissini
Mediterranean Tomato Hummus
Spinach Hummus
Vegetable Crisps

Vicky Jones
Broad Bean & Chicory Dip

Kathy Kordalis
Butter Bean Whip & Crudites Platter
Scorched Aubergine & Cauliflower Dip

Jenny Linford
Broad Bean & Ricotta Dip
Classic Hummus
Roast Garlic Herbed Labneh
Roasted Red Pepper Raita

Dan May
Fresh Aioli
Quick Chilli Lime Mayo
Roast Garlic & Chipotle Mayo

Theo A. Michaels
Red Pepper & Feta Dip
Spicy Remoulade Dip with Crab Fritters
Taramasalata

Hannah Miles
Bagel Toasts
Blue Cheese & Walnut Dip
Cashew & Roasted Tomato Dip
Classic Potato Chips
French Onion Dip
Hawaiian-style Bacon & Pineapple Dip
Homemade Tortilla Chips
Hot Buffalo Chicken Wing Dip
Hot Philly Steak Dip
Layered 'Nacho' Dip
Maryland Crab Dip
Pea, Feta & Mint Dip
Peanut Satay Dip
Ranch Dip
Smoked Salmon, Horseradish & Dill Dip
Spicy Beer Mustard Dip with Maple-Glazed Sausages
Warm Olive & Artichoke Dip

Louise Pickford
Blue Cheese Fondue Dip
Blue Cheese, Garlic & Thyme Dip
Fonduta
Mont D'Or Dip

Milli Taylor
Beetroot Hummus
Marinated Feta Dip
Roast Carrot, Ginger & Miso Dip
Romesco Dip with Grilled Spring Onions
Squid Ink Crackers
Tzatziki
Whipped blue cheese dip

Jenna Zoe
Edamame & Wasabi Dip
Lighter Guacamole
Zesty Almond & Herb Pesto

PHOTOGRAPHY CREDITS

Peter Cassidy
Pages 29, 112.

Helen Cathcart
Pages 6, 13, 22.

Tara Fisher
Page 52.

Richard Jung
Pages 76, 91.

Mowie Kay
Pages 1, 2, 3, 5, 8, 17, 21, 27, 35, 44, 58, 60, 63, 64, 67, 71, 72, 78, 81, 82, 87, 89, 93, 96, 98, 101, 102, 105, 111, 114, 117, 120.

Steve Painter
Page 69.

William Reavell
Page 18.

Ian Wallace
Pages 75, 85, 107.

Claire Winfield
Pages 10, 32, 37, 38, 41, 47, 48, 51, 55, 108.